LUCK!

How to get it
and How to keep it!

LUCK!

How to get it
<u>and</u>
How to keep it!

James Sasse

ELEMENT

CHILDREN'S BOOKS

SHAFTESBURY, DORSET · BOSTON, MASSACHUSETTS · MELBOURNE, VICTORIA

For Jo

Acknowledgements:

Thanks to Barry Cunningham for the encouragement
and to everyone whose writings about luck
have inspired and stimulated me.

First published in the UK in 1998 by Element Children's Books
Shaftesbury, Dorset SP7 8BP

Published in the USA in 1998 by Element Books, Inc.
160 North Washington Street, Boston, MA 02114

Published in Australia in 1998 by Element Books Ltd for
Penguin Books Australia Ltd, 487 Maroodah Highway,
Ringwood, Victoria 3134

Text © James Sasse 1998
Illustrations © Paddy Mounter 1998
Astrological information courtesy of Terri King

The moral rights of the author and illustrator have been asserted

British Library Cataloguing in Publication data available.
Library of Congress Cataloging in Publication data available.

ISBN 1 90188 12 1

Cover design by Ness Wood
Cover picture Telegraph Colour Library
Text design by Dorchester Typesetting Group Ltd
Printed and bound in Great Britain by
Biddles Limited, Guildford and King's Lynn

CONTENTS

Introduction

Consider the following examples of the effect of luck on people's lives:

In 1981, in Smyrna, USA, a man had just taken delivery of his first motorcycle. He invited his best friend round to see his new purchase and decided to demonstrate the new machine in action. He cranked the engine and it roared into life, whereupon the motorcycle shot through some sliding glass doors, dragging its owner with it. While they waited for the ambulance to arrive the man's wife mopped up the spilled fuel with kleenex and threw it down the toilet. When the would-be motorcyclist returned from hospital, covered in bandages, he staggered into the bathroom to sit and reflect on the day's events. While there he smoked a cigarette and then dropped it down the toilet. The explosion that followed threw him through the bathroom door and his wife had to call the second ambulance of the day to carry him back to hospital.

Miss Elvita Adams decided that 1979 would be the year that she ended her own life. Having made up her mind to commit suicide, she went off to the Empire State Building in New York and climbed up to the 86th floor. Having said "goodbye cruel world," Elvita leapt out, only to find that a freak gust of wind blew her back through an open window where she found herself alive and well and on the 85th floor of the Empire State Building.

For most of us the intrusion of good or bad luck into our lives may not be as dramatic as the above examples but it is still often a baffling experience. Luck can come in so many varieties: it can be the straightforward disastrous, spoil-your-day kind or the totally extraordinary, change-your-life kind plus all the variations in between.

People from all over the world have umpteen different strategies to deal with it. But no one seems to have cracked it – so far. Until, of course, this book came along. I am going to approach the whole question in a surprisingly methodical way, at least to begin with. We need to work out what luck is and isn't, if you can just get it, what you can do to hold on to it, and how to deal with bad luck, among other things. But before any of that we need to start with *you*, because what luck means to you depends on what *you* are like.

Consider yourself

Y ou already know a fair amount about yourself: what you look like, what you're good at, what you find difficult, what you're like when you're nice and what you're like when you're nasty.

But how much do you know about how *lucky* you are?
Maybe you're the type that goes for the big statement: "Me? Yeah, I'm lucky," or the all-embracing: "You see? Nothing ever goes right for me."

Or maybe you like to break your luck down into more manageable chunks:

"I'm lucky 'cause I'm not Brad/Emma/the dog."

"I'm lucky 'cause I haven't got bad breath (today)."

"I'm lucky in exams."

"I'm always lucky when it doesn't matter."

"Whenever I tell lies I'm always caught out."

It seems to me that the more time you spend looking at – or looking for – luck, the more luck is not mainly something that *happens* to us but in fact is a part of who we *are*.

When you're sitting in the wreckage left behind by a particularly devastating piece of bad luck you may not want to hear that you are in some way responsible for the bad luck that comes your way.

On the other hand when everything has fallen effortlessly into place and you're feeling witty, cool and good-looking, AND everyone wants to know you, all at the same time, isn't it exciting to think that not only might we have had something to do with this happening, but that we might be able to make it happen again?

So how do I learn about my relationship with luck?

To do this, the best place to start is with what is unique to you; that's to say your name, your body, and the date and time of your birth.

For thousands of years people have experimented with different systems to try to understand more about the pattern of events in an individual's life.

Think of just about anything, and someone somewhere will have tried to build a system around it. For some people freshly-killed chicken's innards contain a mass of information about future luck; for others important decisions can only be made by consulting the dot or the "y" on the end of a cut banana!

Systems come and go but a few have survived and continue to have widespread appeal. Many of these relate to what is particular about you and are meant to tell you more about what may be the right choices at particular points in your life.

For the lazier among us, long-range forecasting of our lives can be a bit energy-sapping. If we work out all our particular information and apply the system, and it says we will be mildly successful in life as a traffic cop, live on our own, never travel, and collect matchboxes as a hobby – the temptation might be to go back to bed and stay there until it's all over.

But divining or predicting systems aren't meant to tell us *exactly* what's going to happen in our lives. First, the information we get is usually quite cryptic, and secondly, it's up to us to interpret it and put it together with what we know about ourselves. That's where luck comes into it, when we make the right choices which suit us, and lo and behold things go well/brilliantly/ecstatically/etc.

For us to understand more about our own luck we have to be prepared to really look at what sort of people we are and concentrate on the divining system we may be using. If we really concentrate on something, it's amazing what can happen. We all know how hard it is to put something out of our minds. Many of us have been in the position of the woman meeting her prospective father-in-law for the first time. The man is stunningly and completely bald, except for a few threads of hair scraped carefully over the top of his head. "I must *not* must *not* talk about hair," thinks the woman. She manages it all through the meal until the last course. For a moment her concentration wavers and, as she passes him the creamer, her subconscious kicks in to make her say: "Would you like some hair with your pudding?"

Test it out for yourself: next time you're involved in a really serious, formal situation try telling yourself *not* to think about jelly/farting/banana skins or whatever and see what your mind gets up to.

So, your mind is in gear, ready to focus on luck; the next step is to explore the systems that can help you get luckier.

Forget about math . . . why numbers are really exciting

You've probably already spent a lot of time studying what numbers *do* when you put them next to one another, turn them upside down or inside out, and generally torture them in other ways; but have you spent much time looking at what numbers *mean*?

People have been excited about what numbers might *mean* for thousands of years. The Chinese, the Egyptians, and the Romans all had different numerological systems but the system that most people still use today comes down to us from the Greeks and from one Greek in particular: Pythagoras. Pythagoras was a philosopher as well as a mathematician and although he did do a lot of math when he was around, in the sixth century BC, he also did a lot of thinking about numbers. Pythagoras came to the conclusion that the whole universe was ordered mathematically and so *anything* in the universe could be expressed in terms of numbers. From this point it's just a small step to say that if everything can be *expressed* as a number then everything can be *understood* as a number.

Why do people get excited about it?

Since Pythagoras people have persisted with numbers because they seemed to work for them and because they recognized the patterns of numerical cycles all around them. American native peoples probably didn't know much about Pythagoras but some of them evolved their own system of numbers. The Sioux believed that 4 and 7 were lucky numbers. When you multiply 4 and 7 you get 28 and in Sioux society 28 was visibly an important number. It was all around them; the moon took 28 days to complete its cycle, and 28 was also the number of ribs on a buffalo, the animal that they depended on and revered. Not surprisingly the Sioux considered 28 to be deeply lucky and they always put 28 feathers in their headdress before going into battle.

The way that numbers occur in our lives is still compelling stuff for many people today. Take the Beard family from Gosport, England. The latest member of the family is baby Emily who arrived at 12 minutes past 12 o'clock on the 12th day of the 12th month (December). Unusual, to say the least, but wait until you look at the rest of the family: her father was born on the 4th day of the 4th month, her mother was born on the 10th day of the 10th month, and her brother popped out on the sixth day of the sixth month. Weird.

So how do you work out your own lucky numbers?

The first number you can work out relates to your birthdate. First of all write out your full birthdate; it doesn't matter if you put the month or the day first in the sequence.

Once you have written them down add all the numbers together, until you end up with only one digit left.

EXAMPLE: how to work out a birthdate number

*Bill Clinton's Birthday is: August 19, 1946,
so 19.08.1946 leaves you adding*

$$1 + 9 + 0 + 8 + 1 + 9 + 4 + 6 = 38 = 3 + 8 = 11 =$$
$$1 + 1 = 2$$

So by keeping adding numbers together you end up with a single digit, in this case **2**.

This number is important; it comes from your birthdate, so as with astrology it should reflect some fairly central things about your character. Numerologists call this the birth number or life path number. The characteristics portrayed by this number are meant to show your direction in life, opportunities that will come your way, and the talents and characteristics that you have to help these things happen.

Which all sounds incredibly positive and exciting but what does it mean to be a 2 or a 4 or a 7? Well, numerologists all have slightly different interpretations of what it is to be a 1 or a 3 or whatever. They do seem to agree though on the core qualities, which are as follows.

Number 1 – The Leader

If you're a 1 it seems you are a natural leader and very individual. Your school reports will be full of words like resourceful, resolute, capable, and determined. You will be able to focus on things and go after them with single-minded determination.

Good points: independent, self-reliant, ingenious; makes things happen; is prepared to seek out the new; has plenty of drive and determination.

Not so good points: can be very impatient, reluctant to accept or learn from criticism, selfish; may not appreciate his or her own achievements; can be inconsiderate of others in the urge to succeed.

Day of the week: Sunday

Color: Red

Famous Number 1s: Mikhail Gorbachev, Martin Luther King

Number 2 – The Diplomat

Number 2s seem to be gifted at everything to do with cooperation; they're good at working in a team, at getting the best out of others, they consider the feelings of those around them.

Good points: good at using their emotions, sociable; good at resolving disputes, able to inspire others; have a natural sense of timing and when to act.

Not so good points: can find it impossible to

make decisions; sees everyone's side of things; can be over-sensitive, prefer fantasy to reality.

Day of the week: Monday

Color: Orange

Famous Number 2s: Diana Ross, Bill Clinton

Number 3 – The Performer

3s seem to be full of enthusiasm and make others around them feel good. They are attracted to laughter, entertainment of some form, and having a good time. They are often lucky with money, and find it easy to attract wealth.

Good points: Can be cheerful, creative, eloquent; good at entertaining others, at making things happen, and at moving and inspiring others.

Not so good points: can get bored and restless very quickly; can be very extravagant with money; can be insecure and jealous; can go down as fast as they went up.

Day of the week: Tuesday

Color: Yellow

Famous Number 3s: F Scott Fitzgerald, Alfred Hitchcock

Number 4 – The Builder

4s are steady, reliable types who will always get the job done. They are very industrious but like to work to a plan, not make sudden decisions or take unnecessary risks.

Good points: 4s are very loyal, dependable, ordered, able to go without things to reach their goal. They're not afraid of putting in the effort, and they make deep and faithful friends.

Not so good points: 4s can be boring, stubborn, and resistant to change. 4s can end up as workaholics and never know when it's time to stop.

Day of the week: Wednesday

Color: Green

Famous Number 4s: Clint Eastwood, Margaret Thatcher, Arnold Schwartzenegger

Number 5 – The Player

5s love anything new and when conditions change they can adapt instantly. They can often be good at a number of things at once and tend to be popular and good communicators. They have a young and competitive approach to life and situations.

Good points: 5s are versatile and quick to learn new skills. They tend to be attractive and charismatic to others. They are adventurous and curious about new people and places while also being very tolerant of others. 5s can work well under stress.

Not so good points: Can be easily distracted; find it difficult to ask for help; find it difficult to be a part of a team. 5s can also become very self-indulgent and impatient when things aren't going so well.

Day of the week: Thursday

Color: Blue

Famous Number 5s: Andre Agassi, Mick Jagger, Adolf Hitler

Number 6 – The Teacher

6s are excellent partners and team members; they're very responsible and fair in judging events or situations. They can be very creative and have the ability to teach.

Good points: Very dependable, serious about responsibilities, loyal to friends, tolerant and unselfish. Honest and able to use intelligence and imagination. Not only motivated by money and success.

24

Not so good points: Can interfere too much in others' lives, find it hard to see things as others may do. Can become anxious and obsessive about small details. Tendency to over eat.

Day of the week: Friday

Color: Indigo

Famous Number 6s: Meryl Streep, Glenda Jackson, James Sasse

Number 7 – The Loner

7s tend to work best on their own; they're often deep thinkers and can also be very intuitive. They can come up with new and revolutionary ideas and can also have the gift of healing others.

Good points: 7s are good at analyzing and using their intuition to work out problems or new ways of doing things. Can be good public performers. Rebellious by nature, they are good at searching out the new, both materially and spiritually.

Not so good points: 7s

ignore advice from others, can spend too much time in a fantasy world. 7s can be secretive and unwilling to share their ideas. Their manner can make them appear arrogant.

Day of the week: Saturday

Color: Violet

Famous Number 7s: Diana, Princess of Wales, John F. Kennedy, Winston Churchill

Number 8 – The Achiever

8s are strong, determined, achievers. They are good at organizing and getting what they set out for. 8s' lives can swing between extremes. They are self-reliant themselves but enjoy helping others.

Good points: 8s are strong and courageous and tend to believe in themselves and their ability to get what they want. Good at planning and working at things over a long period.

Not so good points: Can be ruthless and greedy, dominate everyone around them, neglect friends and family for work.

Day of the week: No special day

Color: Silver

Famous Number 8s: Saddam Hussein, Nancy Reagan.

Number 9 – The Humanitarian

9s can lead extraordinary lives. The number 9 contains all the other numbers within it, so the potential of this number can be enormous. 9s are into ideals and the big questions of life, and tend to care deeply about other people's feelings.

Good points: Can be brilliant at showing others a vision of what is possible and inspiring supporters. 9s tend to be tolerant and very compassionate. Can be very artistic and creative.

Not so good points: Can be temperamental and lose temper easily. Can be impatient and impractical, and can become disconnected from reality.

Day of the Week: No special day

Color: Gold

Famous Number 9s: Mahatma Gandhi, Shirley MacLaine

What next?

So, you've added up the numbers of your birthdate, have reduced them to a single number, and have looked at your very own birth number/life path number and marveled at how exactly the descriptions of the number and its good points match up to all the qualities that you have and show in everyday life. Probably.

Now what? Well, with numerology, the number that you get from your birthdate is the most important one but it's not the only one that matters. So you need to do some more calculations . . .

Your birthday number

This does not require much calculation: if your birthday falls on or between the 1st and the 9th of any month, then it's easy – that's your birthday number.

Example:

James Sasse (Remember him? Yes that's right, he's one of the famous people with a life path number of 6, and coincidentally the person who wrote this book.) . . . James's birthday is August 7th so his birthday number is 7.

If your birthday is a number in *double* figures then you add the two numbers together until you are left with a single figure.

Example:

Birthday 10th = 1 + 0 = Birthday number 1

Birthday 19th = 1 + 9 = 10 = 1 + 0 = Birthday number 1

Birthday 27th = 2 + 7 = Birthday number 9.

So now you have a birthday number. What does it tell you? Your birthday number relates to you as the world sees you. It tells you about the way you behave in everyday situations, which bits of you you are most comfortable with and happy to show to others. If you work out your birthday number and check back to the descriptions given for the numbers 1–9 you should be able to recognize a lot of your characteristics in the description. Your birthday number can of course be the same as the life path number that you calculated from your whole birthdate.

So have a good look at the qualities that come with your birthday number. If it's the same as your life path number then lucky you, you would seem to be literally a quite "together" person already. Most of us have two different numbers. Numerologists regard the life path number as the really important one. This is the direction that we should follow in our lives. The birthday number tells us a bit more about abilities and strengths that we can use. But it is no good focusing on the qualities of the birthday number unless they help us to follow the direction of the life path number.

Is that clear? No? Well in my case my life path number is 6 but my birthday number is 7. If I look at the admirable, good points about the number 7, I can recognize a lot of me in them. I work well on my own, am intrigued by finding new and wonderful ways of being or thinking or doing, tend to be rebellious, etc., and of course am a warm and wonderful human being.

However, if I concentrate on doing all that and ignore all the stuff that comes up for me under Number 6, like being creative and teaching, etc., then according to the numerologists I won't get where I'm meant to be going on my life path and may find life difficult and frustrating.

So, assuming your two numbers are different, you need to take a good look at your life path number and then think how the qualities of your birthday number could complement it.

How to turn your name and other letters into numbers

Once you've mastered your significant dates and turned them into numbers you can take a look at your name. All the letters of the alphabet have a

numerical value and most popular forms of
numerology agree on the values in the table below.

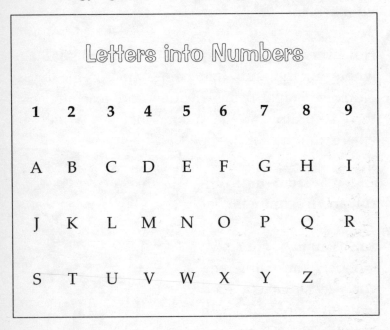

Using these you can turn your name into a number,
for example:

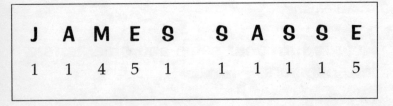

What you get will obviously not be any use as an
alternative name (Try going up to the next stranger

you meet and saying "Hello, you don't know me but I'm One, One, Four, Five One."), but it does give you more numbers that are particular to you. With these you can add them together as you did previously until you are left with a single figure.

Things you can do with your name

First of all write out the first and family names that you are normally known by. If you use any middle names or initials normally then include them; if you don't, don't. Then write out all the number values of the letters as I've done above. Now you're ready to take your name apart and see what it can tell you.

Your vowel number [A, E, I, O, U]:

To get this take the values of all the vowels in your first and second names and add them together to give a single number. Look at the qualities that go with this number on pages 19–27. Your vowel number is meant to give you insights into what motivates you.

Your consonant number [the rest of the letters]:

Again take the values of all the consonants in your names and add them together. This single number should tell you what impression others have of you the first time they meet you.

Your whole name number:

By adding all the values of the letters in your name you get your whole name number. This number tells you more about how you communicate and relate to others.

YOU LOOK LIKE A VOWEL NUMBER 8 TO ME. AM I RIGHT?

What else can you do with letters/numbers?

Part of the usefulness of numerology and other systems that are meant to give you information about you is just that. If you look at what the system is telling you and work out whether it seems right to you or not, you will be spending time thinking about what makes you you and where your strengths and weaknesses are. If you do that on a regular basis, you are going to make better or more useful choices. And if what you choose is best suited to who you are then things will tend to work out better, or you could say you will be *luckier.*

So that's part of why numerology is useful, because you learn about yourself, but you can use numbers in loads of other ways too. Any name or word that matters to you can be translated into numbers. You can then look at the spread of numbers and compare it to something else, e.g.

R	O	M	E	O		J	U	L	I	E	T
9	6	4	5	6		1	3	3	9	5	2

Uh uh, these names don't look so good together. Romeo adds up to a 3, but Juliet adds up to a 5. If we do a bit more work on the vowels and consonants we could say something about how the relationship might work out. But we'd need to go back to the Shakespeare to check out other names, and getting birthdates is going to be a bit tricky . . .

Apart from checking out how two names go together, you can analyze your friends or maybe people you know whom you are *considering* as possible friends. You could get their birthdates and name details and crunch up all the data and work out whether Zoe would be lifelong partner material or Barry would be a no no to share a tent with . . . but remember, if you do this with every person you know and before making every decision, you will lose the element of *spontaneity.*

Any word can be reduced to a number value. You can experiment here to see if the names of people, places, or things that you like/work well with have anything in common with your special numbers. If they do then you could use this system on other words or names that come up for you.

Straight numbers can also be reduced. Any date,

whether it be today's date or the day of your first exam or the next Friday the 13th can be written out in full and reduced to a single value:

April 1st 1999 would be 1.4.1999
so $1 + 4 + 1 + 9 + 9 + 9 = 33 = 3 + 3 = 6$

So April 1st 1999 is a Number 6 day; if your life path number or birthday number is 6 then go for it, you never know what may come up for you.

This is just an introduction to what numbers can do for your luck. Try it out and see what makes sense for you; do you recognize the numbers that your birthdate throws up, or do you see yourself as more of a 1 when apparently you're a 9? If numbers seem to work for you there are lots of other things you can do with your particular numbers.

5

Other things you can do with your birthdate - luck through the stars

Astrology

Probably the best known system for divining our future that uses our birthdate is Astrology. Like numerology, astrology can help us to understand a lot more about ourselves, things we are good at or avoid, and so on. The more knowledge we have about ourselves, the better we are at making lucky choices. Astrology can also guide us to times and dates when we are more likely to be at our best and therefore "luckier".

I'm a Leo, you're a Leo, but we're completely different!

People sometimes get put off astrology because they say how can one small paragraph in the paper or a magazine really be accurate for all the millions of Leos or Virgos or whatever in the world. My wife and I are both Leos but we are very different both as people and in terms of the patterns in our lives.

I'm this sort of Leo

To use astrology as it was intended, what you need to concentrate on is what is unique about you and that is the date, place, and time that you were born. Once you pass all that information to an astrologer you can get a much fuller picture of what your potential and characteristics are.

As a first step you may know what sign you are but you can learn much more about being, say, a Leo if you break down the 30 or so days covered by each sign into 3 periods. This is one of the things that astrologer Terri King does in her books and by checking your birthdate it's quite easy to see which *sort* of Leo you might be, which in turn gives you far more information. So, what sort of Aries/Capricorn/Scorpio or whichever are you?

AQUARIUS (January 21 to February 19)

Early Aquarians, born between January 21 and January 30

Aquarians born in this part of the sign will probably have lots of brainpower and a mind that is always whirring away. You're extremely curious not to say nosy, and you have the ability to get involved in lots of different areas at the same time. You're better at thinking of ideas and ways to sort out problems, so it's a good idea to team up with someone who likes *doing* things otherwise there may not be much to show for all your thinking. You will probably be very sociable but also able to detach yourself and go off into your own world when you feel the need. This sort of Aquarian often has a rebellious streak and may get into battles with authority!

Middle Aquarians, born between January 31 and February 9

This sort of Aquarian will be very good at analyzing and may particularly like math and science. Your mind may work too fast sometimes for your speech or writing to keep up, but what you like best is talking about your ideas and being able to get them across to others. You are generally optimistic and determined, and so when life gives you a kick you are good at accepting it and bouncing back again. You can be quite impatient and prefer to be up and making things happen rather than sitting back and letting events unfold.

Late Aquarians, born between February 10 and February 19

The most sensitive of all Aquarians, you may find it impossible to stay in one place for long. You are drawn to excitement and change. What you're like and what you want can change quite rapidly, which can make you a bit of a mystery to others, and to yourself! Probably a keen thinker, you'll have strong ideas about what's right and wrong and what would make the world a better place. A liking for jumping into situations with both feet may get you into confrontations, but your unusual sense of humor and charm ideally will keep you out of trouble.

FAMOUS AQUARIANS:
James Dean, Mozart, Charles Darwin

 PISCES (February 20 to March 20)

Early Pisceans, born between February 20 and March 1

Early Pisceans tend to be great romantics. You want

life to be dramatic, poetic, and beautiful! You probably have great artistic and creative ability and if there's a choice you'll go for anything to do with feelings and the heart rather than the practical or everyday. If things aren't going your way you may spend too much time hiding away from others and chewing over things. But remember, if you're going to use all that creativity then it's important that you don't spend too much time doing this.

Middle Pisceans, born between March 2 and March 11

Middle Pisceans tend to be considerate, caring, and imaginative. Although you can be quite happy to wander round with your head in the clouds, you also have the ability to make your dreams become reality. As well as all that energy and intelligence you also have a LAZY side. You will need to prod yourself sometimes to remember not to doze off on life! You are also someone who enjoys and goes looking for the pleasures of life, so you need to balance this "ability" of yours with a bit of self-discipline as well. But as long as you can keep getting out of bed *and* encouraging your practical side, you're sure to make an impact.

Late Pisceans, born between March 12 and March 20

For those of you born in this part of the sign, a lot of life may seem to be one change after another. Apart from the usual growing up and learning, you seem to get more than your fair share of upheaval, moving about, and new beginnings. Although you don't enjoy all this change you do seem to have the strength to cope with it, and you're good at taking advantage of what change can bring. Everyone has to cope with the fact that life never stays still and all your experience will make you a bit of an expert. Things tend to go best when you remember to look ahead to what is coming rather than behind at what you are leaving.

FAMOUS PISCEANS:
George Washington, Michelangelo, George Harrison

 ## ARIES (March 21 to April 20)

Early Aries, born between March 21 and March 30

Those born in this part of Aries will have a great

urge to end up on top of the pile. You will probably be very determined and single-minded when it comes to goals. You may trample on others to get where you're going, but the chances are you *will* get there. Courage is not a problem and you will not be frightened to ask, or demand, what you want in life. If you do end up flat on your face, the experience won't put you off; this sort of Aries recovers quickly and won't be put off by failure. With all this aggression and determination you probably won't be the most tactful or diplomatic of people but others will admire your honesty and commitment.

Middle Aries, born between March 31 and April 10

Like the early Aries you are a determined achiever, but this part of the sign suggests more passion and emotion as well. You've got plenty of energy to get you where you want to be. You also have a great talent for organizing things, and other people! You find it easy to throw yourself into whatever is your latest project and others may find it hard to keep up with your work-rate. Your pride and determination to succeed can get in the way of friendship though. It is useful for this sort of Aries to learn to let others get what they want as well from time to time.

Late Aries, born between April 11 and April 20

Late Aries people tend to be more light-hearted and fun-loving and less ambitious than those born under the other parts of Aries. You will be attracted to travel and be very interested in people from other cultures and their lifestyles and customs. You enjoy thinking, learning, and acquiring knowledge. Your sense of humor and charm makes you popular and will often help you get where you want to be in life. You tend to find it much too easy to spend money but you also tend to have a lot of luck in attracting money to make up for it. Your personality will attract friends and good luck in life.

FAMOUS ARIES:
Elton John, Leonardo Da Vinci, Diana Ross

 TAURUS (April 21 to May 21)

Early Taureans, born between April 21 and May 1

Early Taureans tend to be very persistent, kind-hearted, and loyal. You're not one for taking risks and enjoy order and security around you. You can be VERY stubborn especially if you are pushed into a corner, so it's a good idea to warn your friends about this! Many early Taureans have artistic ability and appreciate beautiful things. You may find any sort of change difficult and you may see things in terms of extremes (best friend/worst enemy, greatest essay ever/total disaster, etc.). If this sounds like you, you could try being a bit more flexible; but then, if you succeed you won't be a typical early Taurean!

Middle Taureans, born between May 2 and May 11

Taureans in this section tend to be quite shy and reserved. You like to work things out on your own and rely on logic and brainpower to do it. You are very organized and good at planning things in great detail. Numbers and pages of figures hold no fear for you; in fact, you're a bit of a human computer and find it easy to crunch data. Although to others you may come across as a bit reserved, you enjoy being thrown together with a whole lot of people and having a chance to discuss things and exchange ideas. You may well have a natural ability for photography/film.

Late Taureans, born between May 12 and May 21

This sort of Taurean may well be more studious and serious than others. You are very responsible and may well end up being put in charge of things because of it. Your personality is reserved but once people get to know you you are the loyalest of friends. You can suffer from being over-anxious. Once you are committed to something you are very disciplined and will see it through. It can be very useful to have a regular hobby which brings out and uses the creative side of you.

FAMOUS TAUREANS:
Saddam Hussein, Jack Nicholson, Catherine the Great

 ## GEMINI (May 22 to June 21)

Early Gemini, born between May 22 and May 31

This sort of Gemini has plenty of brainpower and the gift of self-expression. The combination of the two can make you very good at making your point and persuading others. You like company and are good at making people laugh. You have a tendency to mull over things and may find it hard to stop your brain whirring away after you've made up your mind about something. You need to take enough physical exercise to balance all that brain activity, but you're probably quite lazy when it comes to using your body. Your challenge in life is to learn to be in charge of that impressive brain rather than the other way around.

Middle Gemini, born between June 1 and June 11

This sort of Gemini is very creative, charming, and romantic. You have a natural talent with words and can think on your feet, and you're also good at getting your ideas across in writing. As well as all that you're also a bit of a performer. You may not know it but you're probably good at painting/drawing and music as well. To go with this mass of skills you need a bit of self-discipline and you can be a bit short of this sometimes. Other people probably find you quite magnetic so this, plus your charm, should make up for anything missing in other departments like, say, practicality or attention to detail!

Late Gemini, born between June 12 and June 21

You are a bit different to others in your attitudes

and interests, which can be fun if you don't mind standing out from the crowd. You don't like being restricted in any way and you also need plenty of change and excitement if you are not going to get bored. You can be a bit of a yo-yo, very energetic and inspired one moment and rather flat the next. When you are involved in something, though, you seem able to concentrate – whatever may be going on around you. So, you've got plenty of creativity and brain-power but you need to work on the self-discipline.

FAMOUS GEMINIS:
John F Kennedy, Bob Dylan,
Queen Victoria

 CANCER (June 22 to July 23)

Early Cancerians, born between June 22 and July 2

Early Cancerians are a wonderful combination. On the one hand there is sensitivity, creativity, and lots of artistic potential, and on the other there is plenty of practicality, to make things happen. You may also be very intuitive, finding it easy to know what others are feeling and thinking. Sometimes what you feel can overrule your brain and you can get the wrong end of the stick about something and over-react. Being sensitive can be good and bad news. If you can keep your feet on the ground then your awareness of what you and others feel can be very useful, but if you can't then all those feelings can get too much sometimes.

Middle Cancerians, born between July 3 and July 12

Middle Cancerians are big on secrecy. You are probably very good at keeping others out of parts of your life that you consider private. You can be very imaginative and are also good at relating to what others are feeling. Once you take the plunge and go for something you will tend to see it through. With friends you are extremely loyal but you may hang on to people or situations that in your heart you know aren't good for you. You also have a natural interest in history and collecting things.

Late Cancerians, born between July 13 and July 23

Like other Cancerians you're intuitive and compassionate and you, too, have creative and artistic abilities. Cancerians in this section tend to be less ambitious and to be happy to spend time thinking and/or dreaming. Although you may not be as determined or go-getting as some, you are very adaptable. You are good at heading off in new directions and your tolerance and curiosity can take you to some weird and wonderful places. You can get a bit stuck sometimes and need something or someone to give you a push to make things happen in your life.

FAMOUS CANCERIANS:
Princess Diana, Sylvester Stallone,
Rembrandt

 ## LEO (July 24 to August 23)

Early Leos, born between July 24 and August 4

Leos in this part of the sign are likely to be particularly motivated by pride. You may be proud of yourself and/or what you have done. Once you take something on you tend to go at it non-stop until you get there or reach a point of exhaustion, so bear this in mind when choosing your next project.

You probably find it hard to relax and do nothing, and prefer to be busy and involved. You can be interested in lots of things at once but you also have the practicality to make things happen and get things done.

Middle Leos, born between August 5 and August 15

Humor tends to be important to Leos born between these dates. You will have a natural ability to make people laugh. You probably won't be particularly motivated by money or things, and may be attracted to philosophy and thinking about the big "Why" questions such as "what are we all here for?" and "what does it all mean anyway?" You also can get lots of pleasure from the simple things in life. Other people will tend to come to you to tell you about their problems and you may find yourself as the local "rock" and dispenser of wisdom among your friends.

Late Leos, born between August 16 and August 23

You seem to thrive on activity. The more you do, the more energy you seem to have. You're big on will-power, not to say stubborn; once you decide on something, you're going to get it and you're not

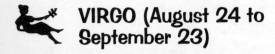

always too fussy about *how*. You're lucky because changes and challenges, which is what life tends to throw at us, are what you enjoy. You seem to thrive on upheaval, and the times in life when you are low and low on energy will probably be when you don't have enough to do.

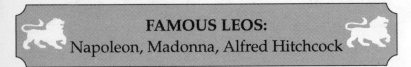

FAMOUS LEOS:
Napoleon, Madonna, Alfred Hitchcock

VIRGO (August 24 to September 23)

Early Virgos, born between August 24 and September 1

Early Virgos are intelligent, logical, and well-disciplined. You are very dependable and hard-working and want to help or serve others. Early Virgos make reliable friends; if you say you'll be there then you will. You tend to be keen on order. You can organize a mass of stuff but still have an eye for the tiny details of whatever it is you're working on. This skill for organizing is valuable but can turn into an obsession; if you find that you're ordering the lives of everyone around you, you know that you've gone too far. When your organizing skills are under control you are usually sympathetic, warm, and generous with others.

Middle Virgos, born between September 2 and September 11

Virgoans born under this section will have great discipline. They also tend to be stubborn and don't give up easily so, not surprisingly, they tend to get things done! You will probably be quite good at acquiring money and possessions and are also good with people and getting others to enjoy themselves when you have a party. On the down side, you can be a bit of a snob about whom you'll hang out with and can be inclined to dwell on the things that are wrong with your life and forget about the good things. More positively, though, you will probably be charming and comfortable in most situations.

Late Virgos, born between September 12 and September 22

Virgos in this section tend to be hard-working and motivated and able to push themselves to get what they want. Your only problem is that you often feel that if you are going to do something it has to be done perfectly. This sort of attitude can make you anxious and tense and can also be a bit of a nightmare for those around you! You'll probably find that if you lower your sights a bit life gets a lot easier. Late Virgos have quite a lot of the performer in them and are also good at inspiring others to take part and get involved in some sort of show or activity.

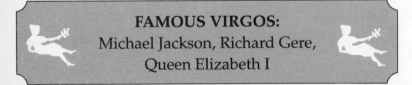

FAMOUS VIRGOS:
Michael Jackson, Richard Gere,
Queen Elizabeth I

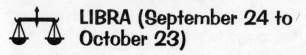 LIBRA (September 24 to October 23)

Early Librans, born between September 24 and October 3

This sort of Libran is highly artistic and creative with a vivid imagination. He or she is also inclined to be soppy and likes a bit of romance. You have a natural ability to see both sides of an argument/situation, so you often end up being the peacemaker. Intellectually you are very good at seeing things in different ways and have a real gift for understanding how others may feel or view things. If you can use these skills and still make decisions that's great and you have an unusual skill; unfortunately this sort of Libran can be so good at seeing both sides of everything that he or she can't ever make his or her mind up!

Middle Librans, born between October 4 and October 13

This tends to be the most serious type of Libran. He or she will probably have strong ideas about right and wrong and what would make the world a better place. A middle Libran will probably have natural musical and acting ability. Something to watch out for is a tendency to take yourself too seriously. If everyone is telling you to lighten up then give it a go, try to see the funny side of things and be more light-hearted. You may be a bit on the serious side but as far as friends and family go you tend to care very deeply about those who are close to you.

Late Librans, born between October 14 and October 23

If you were born in this section you will have a strong, logical mind and a strong sense of justice. You will also be sociable and find it easy to get on with all sorts of people. Late Librans tend to be gifted with words and languages. You'll find it easy to keep up a flow of ideas when talking, and people will tend to find you persuasive, so words will help you to get what you want. Your good sense of humor and loyalty will bring you plenty of friends and, for all your love of chatter, your methodical approach means that you get things done as well.

FAMOUS LIBRANS:
Michael Douglas, Bruce Springstein,
John Lennon

SCORPIO (October 24 to November 22)

Early Scorpio, born between October 24 and November 2

Early Scorpios are often very ambitious and determined to succeed. You have the sort of brain that is cunning and good at digging out information, especially if it is hidden. You are also quite secretive so, if you had the inclination, you would make a very good spy! You like competitive games and find it hard to resist a challenge. When you are involved in something you tend to be very organized, able to put everything else to one side, and prepared to go without things if it helps you to achieve your goal. You may also find that other people find you magnetic and that it's easy to get others to do what you want!

Middle Scorpio, born between November 3 and November 13

This sort of Scorpio is keener on planning and calculating things than doing them! Creatively you are very talented, with musical and writing ability but you may find it difficult to use your talents practically or get others to recognize them. You enjoy excitement and are always looking out for things to spice up life or give you a thrill. Although you can be a bit of a dreamer you also have healing ability, and if you develop your healing skills you could end up helping yourself and others greatly. You will probably be most successful when you're really involved with others and not spending too much time fantasizing about the future.

Late Scorpio, born between November 14 and November 22

The late Scorpio particularly enjoys looking after others, but is not always good at letting others look after them! You are probably more sensitive than Scorpios born under the other sections. Feeling

secure and having strong friendships are probably more important to you than "things" or being a success. Although you are not always very interested in money you will probably have the sort of mind that is quite shrewd at making money if you choose to use it that way.

FAMOUS SCORPIOS :
Pablo Picasso, Marie Antoinette,
Prince Charles

 # SAGITTARIUS (November 23 to December 21)

Early Sagittarians, born between November 23 and December 2

Typically you will have plenty of intelligence and like to do things quickly. You have a great sense of humor which helps you to put up with any of the bad bits that life puts in your path. You like faraway places, adventures, and people that make you laugh. You seem to have unlimited energy and as well as travel you will probably be really into sports. In total you seem pretty easygoing, ready to get the most out of life, popular with just about everyone . . . and you don't have any obvious bad points. (Who said life wasn't fair?)

Middle Sagittarians, born between December 3 and December 12

You're a go-getting, spur-of-the-moment, action-packed person. You find it hard to focus on one thing for long. Usually when you start on something new you pile in there to get things going but may run out of steam before the end. You will be mad about sports and may be one of those demi-gods who can be good at several sports at the same time. You also like to take risks and, with all that energy and enthusiasm, when things work out for you the results will probably be spectacular. You will probably be attractive to others and popular with everyone and you haven't got a mean bone in your body. (What *is* it with Sagittarians??)

Late Sagittarians, born between December 13 and December 21

This type of Sagittarian seems to be as wonderful as the others but with added determination and will-power! The late Sagittarians have a great urge to express themselves and their creativity and they've also got lots of ambition, courage, hope, faith, and patience! They are also organized and disciplined, so they don't run out of steam halfway through things. You're probably already the sort of person that other people notice when you walk into a room and your warmth, energy, and humor make you pretty popular. With all these assets you could end up being successful at just about anything . . . and there still don't seem to be any bad points.

 FAMOUS SAGITTARIANS:
Beethoven, Christina Onassis,
Winston Churchill

CAPRICORN (December 22 to January 20)

Early Capricorns, born between December 22 and January 1

This sort of Capricorn can be quite serious, disciplined and hard-working. What your friends and other people think of you will probably matter to you quite a lot. Once you are friends with someone you tend to be devoted. You will have lots of common sense and the ability to make things and get things done. Because of this you find dreamy, changeable types quite irritating, so try not to get stuck in a partnership with this sort of person, or he or she will really wind you up. You tend to be drawn to those who are at the top of whatever pile you find yourself in, and will probably end up on top of the pile yourself, in time.

Middle Capricorns, born between January 2 and January 11

Middle Capricorns are good with people. You should find it easy to get on with others and they will probably find you charming. You are one of those people who is always coming up with ideas, stuff you've made, things to do; you tend to have lots of energy and don't need much sleep. Unusually, you may be good at passing up pleasure today to reap the benefits at a later date, so you're good at long-term planning. You're also tactful, understanding, sincere, and kind, so you're pretty easy to have around. You can also be VERY stubborn, or enormously determined, depending on which way you look at it. Once you set your sights on something you just keep on going until you get there.

Late Capricorns, born between January 12 and January 20

This sort of Capricorn is full of ideas but may find it difficult to get them across to others. You're probably quite brainy with a strong sense of where you're going and may well be good at creative hobbies. You probably don't like being the centre of attention or telling people exactly what you think about this, that, or the other. But you *have* got plenty of good ideas and plenty to say – you just have to push yourself forward more. Also, while we're handing out the advice, when you make a mess of things don't keep brooding on it, take a deep breath and move on – that way you'll make the most of your abilities.

 FAMOUS CAPRICORNS:
Joan of Arc, Humphrey Bogart,
Sir Isaac Newton

Where astrology gets really interesting

Ideally, you will have recognized some of yourself in the section above that relates to your birthdate; but, if you feel that astrology works for you, you can go a lot further with it. The reason that astrology seems to work for many people is that it works

from a unique "snapshot" of what was going on in the heavens at the time when, and above the place where, you were born. The sign of the zodiac that you are is really just the tip of the iceberg.

What makes you *and your luck* different from every other person who shares your sign is what all the other planets were doing at the exact moment you burst out on this unsuspecting world. For instance, where was the moon when you were born? The moon enters a fresh sign every 48 hours. The sign the Moon was in can tell you a lot about your instincts and ways that you react. Your main, or sun, sign may be one thing but your moon sign could be quite different. Another hugely important part of your astrological profile is which sign was passing over the horizon at the time you were born. These change about every 2 hours and the rising sign, as it's called, determines your personality and how you appear to others.

How to find out more

Luckily it's not vitally important that a parent or relative was perched over a telescope keeping an eye on all the planets as you came kicking and screaming into the world. What you need to know, if possible, is what the local time was when you were born and whereabouts it was geographically. Armed with those bits of information you can contact a real human astrologer or use a computer program to find out what your particular birth chart looks like.

Once we've got a fuller picture we can use astrology to improve our luck in two ways. Like other systems it may tell us a lot more about ourselves, sometimes a lot more than is comfortable to admit to anyone else. I have no problem relating to the attractive, sensitive bits of my birthchart, it's the bits that say things like "may have a tendency to megalomania . . ." that are more difficult to handle. Either way a fuller picture of ourselves, if we recognize it to be true, can help us to make the right choices and realize and deal better with our weaknesses. All of which means less time bemoaning our lack of luck when we attempt something that is really wrong for us and – surprise, surprise – it doesn't come off.

The other way in which astrology can improve our luck enormously is in recognizing cycles that operate in our lives. If astrology works for us it can help us choose the right times to do things in our lives

and give us confidence that this week or whenever is good for me to take risks, attempt something new, or do whatever else the chart indicates. Astrology can be a wonderful guide. It's not meant to tell us everything that's going to happen so that we switch off or give up. What it's meant for is giving us insights into the patterns in our lives and what we are capable of. Learning more about those things can lead to us definitely being luckier, and learning to avoid bad luck. But it *is* a learning process. If you want to know more, Terri King's books, also published by Element, will help you find out a lot more about you, your luck, and astrology.

6

Other bits of you that may affect your luckiness

Get a grip on your hands

Apart from your birth particulars there are other qualities to do with our bodies that may affect our luckiness. In terms of contact with others, our hands are pretty crucial and there's a whole tradition of interpretation about character and future luck built on what our hands look like.

Palmistry is not just something that happens in a darkened booth at a fairground where a wrinkle-faced gypsy lady bends over your sweaty palm and wheezes sweet nothings about life and loves, although it's maybe not a bad place to start if you've never had your palm read before! Anyone can pick up the basics of palmistry and try it out at home or on friends to see if either you're any good at it or if it seems to work for you or your friends.

In spite of people poking fun at the image of "having your hand read", lots of people are still curious about it and many use it on a regular basis. Nobody is quite sure why palmistry should work. A large part of our nervous system runs between the brain and our two hands. Some people feel that this makes the surface of our hands a good place to "read" what's going on in our heads. If you talk to palmists they will all have differences in the way that they interpret hands. As with numerology and astrology, interpretations have built up over many generations, and like them palmistry has gone in and out of favor throughout history. In the 1600s palmistry was being taught at universities in Germany while at the same time it was outlawed in England as a form of witchcraft!

The basic things to look for

First of all, which hand? Well the answer is both. If you are right-handed then your right hand is meant to indicate what you're like now and what your future may hold while your left hand is meant to tell you about the potential that you were born with. If you're left-handed then it will be the other way round.

A skilled palm-reader can deduce an enormous

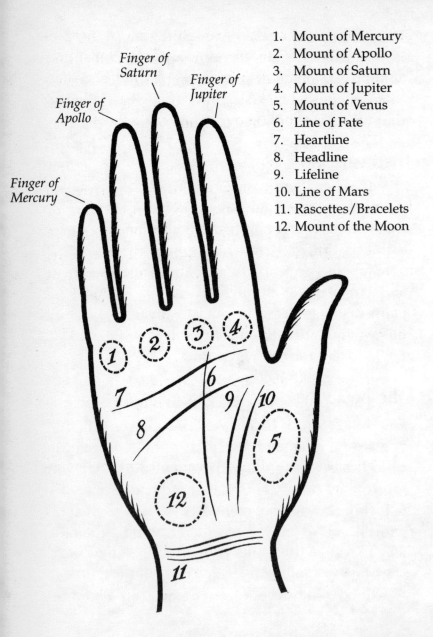

Finger of Saturn

Finger of Jupiter

Finger of Apollo

Finger of Mercury

1. Mount of Mercury
2. Mount of Apollo
3. Mount of Saturn
4. Mount of Jupiter
5. Mount of Venus
6. Line of Fate
7. Heartline
8. Headline
9. Lifeline
10. Line of Mars
11. Rascettes/Bracelets
12. Mount of the Moon

amount from the shape of your fingers, the suppleness of the joints, the condition of the nails, and hundreds of other details. But I am not a skilled palm-reader so I'm just going to stick to some of what the major lines on our hands can tell us!

The head line ⑧

Your head line relates to your mental approach to life. If your head line doesn't seem to be there or looks a bit short, do not panic. This does not mean you're stupid! What's important is the shape of the line and what it's doing in relation to the rest of your hand.

Some common head lines:

Runs straight across the palm: this suggests a practical, methodical person who is good at organizing.

The head line slopes towards the mount of the moon: you are sensitive and imaginative.

The head line runs to the middle of the wrist: you find it hard to keep your feet on the ground.

The head line is sharp and well-defined: you find it easy to concentrate.

The head line is broken up like a chain: poor concentration.

Starts out joined to your life line: can be cautious and find it hard to accept criticism.

Head line ends in a three-pronged fork: you have ability to do well in business, imagination, and intelligence!

Head line ends at mount of Mercury: you have the golden touch for making money.

The life line ⑨

Again, do not panic if you find it hard to find your life line or if yours seems to be a bit wobbly or short. Your life line does NOT tell you how long you're going to live. Your life line gives you information on your level of energy in life, as well as some trends at certain periods of your life.

Some common life lines:

Life line comes and goes: several changes in direction in life.

Starts with headline: cautious and calculating.

Life line has a branch to Mount of Apollo: you will find that people recognize your abilities in life.

Life line has a branch to the Mount of the Moon: you are always on the lookout for new challenges and directions.

Your life line has a branch that joins up with your head line: if this happens halfway along your life line it may mean that you'll be successful in middle age.

Your life line ends in a fork with one side of the fork ending at the mount of the Moon: you will go on long journeys.

Your life line has a branch line up to the mount of Jupiter: you are self-confident and comfortable with others.

The heart line ⑦

This line tells us about our emotions, how we deal with them, and what may happen in our relationships with others.

Some common heart lines:

The heart line is longer and more defined than the head line: your heart will tend to overrule your head.

A very straight heart line: you may find it hard to show your feelings, and may be more interested in yourself than in others!

Your heart line has a branch joining up with your head line: love and work may come together in your life; you may live with someone you work with.

Your heart line starts with a fork on the

mount of Jupiter: you are easy to love and easy to be with and will make someone a good partner.

Your heart line is broken in lots of places: your feelings tend to fluctuate a lot.

The line of fate ⑥

Although it sounds really dramatic the line of fate is actually not as important as the other lines. Many people do not develop a line of fate until later in life. If you do have one it can tell you about challenges and obstacles in your life and give you tips about your strengths and weaknesses.

Some common lines of fate:

Your line of fate starts from your heart line or head line: you will be successful later in life.

Your line of fate is broken with overlapping sections: your life will have several major changes.

Your line of fate curves towards your

mount of Jupiter: success in your life will usually come through effort.

Line of fate that's straight with no gaps: a successful life with few troubles.

A line of fate that starts from the mount of the Moon: changeable life with a lot of travel.

Line of fate ends on the head line: beware of misjudging people or situations.

But what do I do if my lines look like mixed-up spaghetti?

Hands can be pretty confusing: is that my head line or my life line? What if my line of fate turns into a heart line? What if my life line's too far over – does that mean it's something else? If you enjoy palmistry it's worth consulting an expert or spending some time with some specialist books. (See the list at the end of this book.) Navigating your way around the hand can be hard even when you've seen thousands of them, so don't jump to any conclusions the first time you have a good long look at your own sweet palm.

Some hand notes

The shape and markings of your hands can change as you grow and get older, so even if there are omens in your hand that you're not too keen on, don't worry, they *can* change. Also, it's important to have a complete picture of what your hands are telling you. Palm readings are like people, they've got good bits and less good bits and obvious and hidden abilities, and a good reader will be able to give you a balanced picture, not one based on one line or area of the palm.

The man who lost the lines on his hands

Sir Francis Galton was a cousin of Charles Darwin, the famous English scientist. Sir Francis was very interested in how palmistry could be linked to science. In the course of his research he came across a house-painter. The house-painter had fallen off a building and for a week after the accident he was unconscious. During that week all the creases on the man's hands disappeared, but as he slowly regained consciousness so the lines on his hands reappeared.

So keep an eye on your hands; those lines can change! If you want to keep a record you can make a print, by putting a thin film of ink all over the palm and fingers and pressing down evenly on to a piece of paper. A good print can help you compare left and right: work on your own readings and you can see your hands changing over time.

Other ways our body can tell us about luck

Apart from our hands there are other ways that our bodies can tell us things. Many superstitions have built up around involuntary things that our bodies do – like sneezing. In medieval times many cultures believed that if someone sneezed, whatever was being talked about in the conversation at that moment would happen. Most of us don't take the superstition that far nowadays, but a lot of people still make some sort of blessing if someone sneezes. For example, *Gesundheit!*, which is German for "your health!"

Feelings and tingling in the body can be trying to tell us something. There are lots of expressions in our language that recognize this: "I bet his ears will be burning," "I've got itchy fingers," "That sends shivers down my spine." All of these sayings remind us that our bodies are capable of communicating with us in more complicated ways than

just telling us that we are tired or that we really shouldn't have eaten that fourth bit of cake.

So next time you get a funny feeling in your stomach, your arms are suddenly covered in goosebumps, or your heart starts pounding for no reason, don't just ignore it, pay attention and make a note of what you were feeling and what happened next. You might find that, if you get used to listening, your body can help you to attract good luck *and* avoid bad luck.

How to attract good luck and avoid everyday bad luck

S o you've looked through the systems and you've recognized parts of yourself and found some clues to what may be lucky choices or directions for you – we hope. Or maybe you haven't: for some people astrology, numerology, etc. just don't seem to hit the button. If that's the case, don't worry, it doesn't mean that you're lacking in the luck department. It just means that you and luck work differently and there's plenty of other ways to work on that.

Sometimes, in everyday life, just being who you are isn't enough. You want to do something *extra* to bring good luck into your life or you want to know what to do to keep bad luck out. So what can you do to make a difference? You can start with your own personal luck device . . . a talisman.

How to make your own talisman

A talisman is usually something like a stone, a piece of paper, jewelry or anything that can be inscribed with words or figures that *you* believe have special powers. The other thing about a talisman is that you're meant to touch or stroke it, not just carry it around buried in the bottom of a school bag. You can carry a talisman with you, or wear it, or you can attach it to a part of a building, like the door of a room or a house, so that you can touch it when going in and coming out.

Traditional talismans were things like a medal with an image of St. Christopher (patron saint of travelers) on it or the Jewish Mezuzah (a hollow metal tube with a parchment inside inscribed with holy verses) that was nailed to the doorframe of a house. But the point about a talisman is that *you* believe that the thing and the inscription on it are lucky for *you*. So if a packet that says "Salt" and

84

"MacDonalds" on it does that for you then no one can tell you otherwise.

Traditional and modern talismans

If you want to make a really traditional talisman you could come up with your own version of an abraxas stone. These were common in medieval times and were usually stones carved with the Greek word "abraxas." The word represented all the minor gods that Ancient Greeks believed in and the number 365, the number of days in the year. There would also have been a figure of a strange creature made out of a rooster's head (for alertness), a man's body holding a whip and a shield (for power and wisdom), and legs made from two serpents (for spirituality and understanding). Unless you happen to be brilliant at stone-carving you could draw this out on a piece of paper or cloth and put it inside a container such as a pouch or tube.

If you want to use traditional materials to make your talisman, consider using a small piece of wood which can be written or drawn on. In medieval times the following woods were believed to have special qualities:

Alder	Resistant to water and associated with having firm foundations.
Aspen	A wood of protection, a physical or magical shield.
Beech	Used for writing on in the old days, so it's associated with wisdom.
Bramble	A thorny plant and so gives protection.
Holly	Prevents harm coming in, so good for for doorways.
Maple	Associated with long life.
Oak	Strength and protection from lightning.
Pine	Brings light and knowledge.
Rowan	Good for protecting houses.
Willow	Purity and resilience.

Once you've decided what to make your talisman out of, what you put on it is up to you. It could be ancient verses or the lyrics of your favorite song, lucky numbers, lucky symbols, a prayer . . . anything you like.

The only important things are that: *you* make it (it won't be nearly as effective if you buy it from a shop or get someone else to make it) and that you make it out of things that *you* consider to be lucky. For some people their talisman may be a lucky hat or some special bit of cloth-ing. My first talis-man was a plastic troll with orange fur and green eyes that I took to all my exams. (Mind you, this was in the 1970s!)

Everyone else's idea of how to avoid bad luck and attract good, otherwise known as . . . superstitions

Wherever you go in the world people have come up with their own ideas about what's lucky and what's unlucky. To make life more confusing for the would-be lucky person, our ideas about what's lucky don't stay still. Take the swastika: until Hitler adopted it as the emblem of the Nazi party in the 1930s this version of the cross was a potent lucky symbol found in ancient Asian cultures and among the Native Americans. Once the Nazis had got hold of it, the swastika never recovered its former widespread status as a lucky cross.

The other thing that often catches people out is the way that superstitions are often reversed in different places, even within the same country. So how can you navigate through the mass of superstitions that exist without inadvertently doing the wrong thing? Well, the short answer is that you can't, so don't worry about it. My theory, which is totally unscientific, is that:

1 **If you don't know about a superstition then it doesn't apply to you.**

(2) Once someone has pointed out a local superstition to you, it's up to you whether you believe in it or not.

So, there you are, a totally foolproof way of dealing with superstitions! Well nothing in life is really that simple, especially when it comes to luck, but I think it's a good attitude to start off with. In fact superstitions are often intriguing, tied up with history or religion, and if we understand them and believe in them then they can work in our favor.

A random list of my favorite superstitions

Touch wood

This seems to exist in lots of cultures. The knocking or touching wood goes back to the idea that benevolent spirits lived in trees. Most versions of it agree that if we talk about some good thing that we've done or that we're expecting then we are tempting fate or bad spirits to snatch it away from us. The way to avoid this is to touch wood and get the protection of the wood spirits, and as long as we can find something wooden to touch then this is a free and instant form of insurance.

Ladders

This is just plain obvious. Serious books on superstition explain that the ladder makes a triangle with the ground and whatever it's leaning against, and that the triangle is a spiritually significant shape and should not be violated by walking under the ladder. Which may all be true, but loads of people who aren't superstitious avoid walking under ladders too because they would rather not have something fall on their heads.

Black Cats

Black cats are a source of great confusion. The Ancient Egyptians were cat crazy and considered all cats to be sacred to the goddess Isis so they were definitely LUCKY, but it was very UNLUCKY to kill or hurt one. In medieval times it was believed that there were witches who had the power of changing into a black cat, so that therefore a black cat crossing your path was definitely BAD LUCK. From this point the superstition seems to have split in two: black cats are considered to be LUCKY in Japan, North America, Europe, and Scandinavia – unless you happen to be part of a large minority in North America, Europe, or Scandinavia who continue with the medieval view and believe they are UNLUCKY! Is that clear? So next time a black cat crosses your path you know exactly what to do . . . don't you!

Tattoos

In lots of cultures, symbols or drawings cut into or

painted on the skin were meant to be a protection against evil and so bring good luck. Then much later sailors and soldiers decided tattoos were lucky for practical reasons. They thought that if they drowned or were killed in battle and their bodies were mutilated their friends would still be able to tell who they were from their tattoos and so would make sure that they received a proper burial. Which is a good example of how superstitions change and a good reason to wear a tattoo if you like them.

Horseshoes

Most people think horseshoes are good luck and most people seem to agree that you should always hang them with the points upward – to stop the luck running out. Horseshoes are considered lucky because the U-shape or crescent has been a powerful protective sign for centuries and iron was believed to carry good luck. But there is a good story to go with them too. Apparently, St. Dunstan, who was a blacksmith in England, was approached by a dark figure in a cloak. The figure asked him if he would put shoes on him instead of on his horse. St. Dunstan agreed but remembered that the Devil was meant to have hooves and that hooves needed shoes. So he put the shoes on but nailed the Devil to the wall at the same time and poked him with a red-hot poker until he agreed never to enter a house with a horseshoe over the door!

Thirteen

Fear of the number thirteen has been around for years. For the Ancient Egyptians, though, the thirteenth step was the step to eternal life, so for them it was lucky. Thirteen has always been a bit odd; fairly early on people realized that you couldn't do the same things to 13 as you could to all the numbers that came before it, so it was obviously different. Different became bad when Norse mythology came up with the story of a feast of 13 gods and goddesses where Balder the god of beautiful things was killed. And 13 became doubly bad when it was associated with the Last Supper where 13 sat down to eat and one of them betrayed Jesus. On the other hand, let's be fair about this; in Aztec culture 13 was lucky and it's still a lucky number among Buddhists today. For Americans it's also a bit confusing because their flag has 13 stripes on it and on the back of the dollar bill the eagle holds thirteen arrows in one talon and an olive branch with thirteen leaves in the other. So, take your pick: lucky or unlucky or, if it's all a bit too much, just ignore it.

Rodeo superstitions

I've never taken part in a rodeo but I came across some rodeo superstitions and they impressed me with their practicality. Apparently, if you're a rodeo competitor you should:

1. never compete with coins in your pocket
2. always shave before you compete
3. never leave your hat on a bed – if you do, you could be injured or killed.

From what I know of rodeo, if I was going to be thrown off a horse or cow I wouldn't want anything in my pockets and I would want to be clean-shaven if I was going to get a face full of dust. Also if I left my hat on a bed someone, probably me, would be bound to sit on it.

When things have gone terribly wrong - how to break bad luck

Sometimes we do seem to be stuck in a patch of really appalling luck and there is a strong urge to do something to break out of it. At this point, when you're locked out of your house and you've just dropped your keys down a drain, someone usually tells you that bad luck always come in threes. This is not helpful and it's not necessarily so! It tends to be true if you *believe* it to be true, and you're convinced that the sooner the third horrible thing happens the sooner your bad luck will be over.

If you want to break bad luck there are some traditional things you can try:

Spitting

Traditionally spitting was always believed to be a powerful way to stop bad luck, in the form of spirits, coming in through the mouth. To break bad luck combine spitting with the magic properties of the number 3 and turning yourself around as a symbol of reversing your luck. You may be self-conscious about doing this in front of others, but lots of people swear by it. Turn around three times and then spit three times while thinking about changing your luck and see what happens.

St. Jude

He is the patron saint of hopeless causes. This is because although he was one of the original disciples appointed by Jesus people confused him with Judas who betrayed Jesus. Because of the confusion people only prayed to St. Jude after their prayers to all the other saints had failed. So, if you seem to be up against overwhelming bad luck start with St. Jude and offer up a prayer for your luck to change.

St. Anthony

He is the saint of lost things. If your bad luck involves having lost something important then put up a prayer to St. Anthony. A traditional one is:

> *St. Anthony, St. Anthony,*
> *Please come down,*
> *Something is lost*
> *And can't be found.*

St. Anthony seems to exist in different versions in many cultures and is always thought to be able to help recover whatever is lost. So if you haven't tried this, give it a go.

Some of the luckiest and unluckiest people ever

The Birdman of Los Angeles

Larry Waters worked for the US Airforce; his job was on the ground as his poor eyesight disqualified him from flying. But Larry had always wanted to experience flying so one weekend he went to his local Army Surplus shop and bought 45 weather balloons and 5 canisters of helium. In the backyard of his house Larry attached the balloons to his garden chair and the chair to his jeep. When the balloons were filled he found that the chair hovered nicely a few feet off the ground. So Larry collected together beer and sandwiches and his air rifle. The plan was to go up to 50 feet or so and have a look around the neighborhood and when he had had enough he would shoot some of the balloons with the air rifle and drift back down to the ground.

So Larry climbed on to his garden chair and cut the cord that tied the chair to his jeep. The chair, Larry, and the balloons shot straight up into the sky and kept on going until eventually leveling out at 11,000 feet. Larry admitted to reporters that he had felt pretty scared at this point: it was very cold up there and he didn't dare shoot the balloons in case things got even worse. After 14 hours clinging on to his garden chair Larry drifted on to the main approach corridor for Los Angeles International Airport. Air Traffic Control spotted him on their radar and when Larry didn't respond to their radio messages they sent a helicopter up. The helicopter crew managed to get a line to Larry and lift him out of his chair, and the chair and the balloons shot upwards and disappeared from sight.

Hey I won something on the lottery!

If the amount you win decides how lucky you are then Leslie Robbins and Colleen DeVries from Fond du Lac, Wisconsin, USA went off the scale with their lottery win. It came to $111,240,463.10 or £74,353,689.

The chances against that happening are . . .

Once in three million, seventy-two thousand, eight hundred and eighty-seven times. Those were the combined odds a woman from Nottingham beat when she picked five winning horses one after another. Her 5 pence bet returned £153,644.40.

Charles Goodyear and useful rubber

In the 1830s rubber was well known to scientists and industrialists but no one could find a way of overcoming the fact that when it got cold it went stiff and brittle and when it got hot it became soft

and sticky. Charles Goodyear was the poor son of a merchant and inventor in Connecticut, USA. He was obsessed with finding a way to make rubber that didn't change at high or low temperatures. From 1830 to 1839 Charles tried everything and sank all the family's savings into his experiments. Then one day when he was mixing rubber with sulphur he accidentally let the mixture touch a hot stove. To his amazement the rubber didn't melt and Charles realized that he had stumbled on the process that would make rubber stable.

One of the luckiest <u>and</u> unluckiest people

Eduardo Sánchez, a 35-year-old businessman from Barcelona, Spain was in Stockholm, Sweden on business. Eduardo was a Catholic and decided to go into a church in Stockholm to pray. Inside the church was empty except for a coffin and next to the coffin a book of condolence. A sign on the book said that those who prayed for the soul of the departed man should put their names and addresses in the book. So Eduardo did and a few days later returned to Spain. A few weeks later Eduardo got a letter from a Swedish law firm telling him that he was a millionaire. Jens Svenson, the man whose body had been in the church, was a 73-year-old property dealer with no relatives. In his will Jens said that whoever prayed for his soul would inherit his estate and Eduardo was the only one who had.

Unfortunately, though, the reason that Eduardo had gone into the church in the first place was to pray for his own health, as he knew that he had a form of cancer. Once he got back to Spain further tests showed that, although he was now a millionaire, the cancer he had was terminal and the doctors could do nothing to save him.

The unluckiest diamond in the world

The 44.5 carat Hope diamond is the biggest blue diamond in the world and it has also been extremely unlucky for everyone who has ever owned it. Legend has it that it was stolen from an Indian temple and smuggled to France where it became part of King Louis XIV's crown jewels. He gave it to a courtier who soon died, and the stone later fell into the hands of Queen Marie Antoinette who was guillotined. Thomas Hope, an English banker, bought the diamond in 1830, whereupon his family went bankrupt. The next owner, Jaques Colet, killed himself and the one after that, Prince Kanitovitsky, was murdered. Then it was bought by Sultan Abdul Hamed who lost his throne and the diamond to Simon Montharides whose entire family was killed in an accident. Eventually a wealthy Texan lady, Evalyn Walsh, bought it and took it back to America. Evalyn's husband, son, and daughter all died soon after, and finally this terrible jewel ended up in Washington's Museum of Natural History.

Canada's unluckiest bank robber?

DON'T TRY NOTHING FANCY LADY - TAKE THIS $2·600. AND PUT IT ON DEPOSIT.

Gerald Dixon, aged 26, decided rob the Whitby branch of the Bank of Montreal. To prepare for the raid he visited the town's camping store and, on a hot July day, bought a balaclava which he put on and wore on the short journey from the camping store to the bank. The raid was a success but once the camping shop manager heard that $2,600 had been stolen from the bank by someone wearing a balaclava, he was able to show the police footage of Gerald buying his balaclava on the shop's video. Before the police could track Gerald down he turned up, at the bank he had just robbed, this time without the balaclava, and asked to open an account. When he was asked how much he wanted to deposit Gerald replied: " $2,600 cash."

(Actually I'm not sure that bad luck had so much to do with this one.)

Where does luck come from?

Consider the following facts that connect two of America's presidents:

Abraham Lincoln and John F. Kennedy

Each of the names Lincoln and Kennedy has seven letters.

....

Both of them were assassinated on a Friday, in front of their wives.

....

Lincoln was elected in 1860, Kennedy was elected in 1960.

....

Both presidents were succeeded by men called Johnson.

....

Andrew Johnson and Lyndon Johnson: there are thirteen letters in each name.

....

Andrew Johnson was born in 1808, Lyndon
Johnson was born in 1908.

....

John Wilkes Booth and Lee Harvey Oswald
were the two men accused of the killings.

....

There are 15 letters in each name.

....

Booth and Oswald were both murdered before
they could be brought to trial.

....

Lincoln's secretary was called Kennedy,
Kennedy's secretary was called Lincoln.

....

Lincoln's secretary advised him not to go to
the theater, where he was killed.

....

Kennedy's secretary advised him not to go to
Dallas, where he was killed.

I like coincidences. I find the strange similarities
that pop up in the histories of the two presidents
exciting and extraordinary. I enjoy finding things or
events that seem to be related in some impossible or
unlikely way. Often if we follow back a chain of
events we may find that what started off a whole
episode which turned out to be lucky was that we

saw or heard something or someone at just the moment when our brains were looking for a piece of information or an idea. That event set the ball rolling and then this and then that and so on. What is very difficult to work out is how much luck had to do with each twist and turn that ended up with something happening to us that we decided to call lucky.

Rationally we are wonderfully sophisticated human machines and we *make* things happen in our lives. It is we who make the decisions. Which is fine, but it doesn't explain all sorts of things that tend to crop up in our lives, like going to a 20,000-seat stadium and ending up sitting near to someone you haven't seen for five years; or being about to go out the door when you stop because you know the phone is going to ring – and it does. There are so many bits of us and our lives that no one seems to be able to explain satisfactorily. Personally I think this is "a good thing" because if everything could be modeled, and worked out, and replicated, life would lose a lot of its spontaneity. But, since we are all human it is instinctive to want to be able to work out how things happen and be able to make them happen again.

Which is why luck is so baffling. It's often hard to explain and when we *think* we can we're often proved wrong. In a way, luck seems to be all around us and seems almost *visibly* to emerge in our lives from time to time, when we have connected in some way with another person or thing, and then we see what happens next as "lucky."

You may find the paragraph above somewhat vague and wishy-washy; but I think that actually

the quickest way to increase our luckiness is to stop trying to understand luck and concentrate instead on what it is that *we* seem to be doing when luck is working in our lives . . .

How to make your own luck

S o here we are – at the really important part of the book. Forget about all the rest of it, *this* is where I reveal the true secret of how, in the comfort of your own home, you can make all the luck you'll ever need. Well, actually, no . . . I'm not going to do that.

But, I think there *are* some things we can do which may help us to bring luck into our lives and tap into whatever powers may lie behind all the extraordinary coincidences and unexplainable happenings there are in the world.

Expect to be lucky

Top athletes, successful artists, high-profile people in all walks of life tend to use the power of positive thinking. "The power of positive thinking" sounds like something out of an advertisement but the basic idea is simple. If you expect to be lucky, or to have good things happen to you, or to be successful at something, then it is more likely to happen. People who believe in the idea of positive thinking have different explanations for why they think it works. My best guess is that, by focusing our thinking on something good that we want to happen, more of our energy is available to take advantage of whatever else is going on around us to make that thing more likely to happen. Whatever the reason, try it out for yourself and make up your own mind.

It's easy to see the opposite is true. If you know of someone who doesn't get on too well with a certain teacher or in a certain subject you can see what effect the teacher's expectations of that person has on his or her ability. Unfortunately it happens too often that negative thinking along the lines of "Wayne is always disruptive/bad at math/slow" gets communicated from the teacher to poor old Wayne – and the effect is that Wayne ends up *being* how the teacher expects him to be. What you do with your thinking is powerful stuff, either way.

So does that mean all I have to do is be happy and totally positive all the time?

No.

I am not suggesting that you wander around saying "Hello trees, hello sky" and smiling at everyone and everything. There is a difference between having a positive attitude about certain things and getting completely carried away! If, when you think about it, you expect to be lucky I think you will find that you *will* be, more often than you would expect. But even with positive thinking we are not going to be lucky all the time. Things we really want to happen won't, we won't get picked to be in the team, or whatever it is. Then it can be important to take a long-term

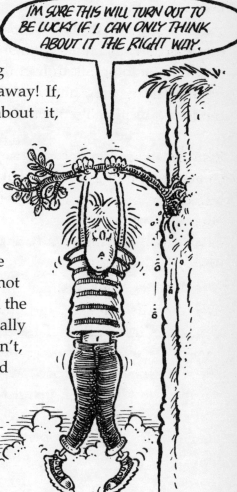

view. Lots of the things that happen to us in our lives can turn out, in the end, to be lucky, but they don't *seem* lucky at the time.

It is worth thinking about things in your own life that turned out differently to how you expected them to. Did something that you thought was lucky turn out not to be? Or did something terrible actually end up by being pretty good news? Luck is not the sort of thing that stands still, and neither are we, so it is important that we keep an eye on how things turn out in the end *and* that we are prepared to change our minds about what's lucky and what's unlucky.

And the third way to make your own luck . . .

Is to follow your instinct. If you have a strong urge that such and such a thing would be lucky for you, then try it. We all have intuitive ideas that come to us and often we ignore them or think they are silly so we don't do anything about it. It *is* worth following your instinct and you may find that it can make you lucky. It's also worth remembering what happens when we do. If you find that you often get a hunch about this or that, try writing down what you felt, what you did about it, and what happened. That way you can see if your instincts are a good guide and you'll probably learn a whole lot more about that side of yourself.

What is your
luck rating?

OK so you've got this far, you've read some/ most/none of the book and you want to test your own luckiness. You need to look at the following questions and pick whichever answer seems closest to what your response might be.

Ready?

1. You're standing in the kitchen, it's too early in the morning, you're half asleep, and the piece of toast that you've just covered with butter and marmalade slips out of your hand. Do you:

a) look down and expect to see it balanced on its side, waiting for you to pick it up?

b) hope that it might have landed sticky side up?

c) assume that it *will* have landed sticky side down, and slam your hand down on the counter thus knocking over your bowl of cereal as well?

2. You're cycling towards a sharp corner in a foreign country when a black cat suddenly runs across the road about ten yards in front of you. Do you:

a) veer off towards the cat calling "Here kitty kitty, here kitty kitty?"

b) slow down in case the cat might mean something lucky or unlucky is about to happen?

c) ride into the ditch and wait there for half an hour in case something horrible was about to happen?

3. You are looking at your palm one day when you suddenly realize that you now have a line of fate on your hand which wasn't there yesterday. Do you:

a) book an appointment immediately with your local palm reader?

b) think "that's odd" and that you must look it up in a book sometime to see what it might mean?

c) start wearing gloves so that you won't see it?

4. One morning you catch your favorite sweatshirt on your bedroom door handle and rip a big hole in it. Then at breakfast you go to pour the milk and miss, and cereal, sugar, and loads of milk end up in your lap. As you're wondering whether to change your jeans, your father walks into the room with a letter in his hand and says "You'll never guess what!" Do you:

a) think "never mind about my soggy crotch 'cause this is bound to be news that we've won the dream family trip to Hawaii?"

b) say "What?"

c) assume that this has got to be something bad, like your school report arriving early, and that it's going to be the third and biggest disaster of the day?

Time to add up your scores: for each answer

a) score 1, *b)* score 2, *c)* score 4.

TOTALS

4–6: You are *very* positive about the role that luck can play in your life but sometimes think that luck can compensate for everything else like not having done your homework, not using your brain, and not paying enough attention to boring old reality.

7–10: You are prepared to accept that good and bad luck can be important in your life but you're not going to let it dominate. You tend towards the optimistic but you're not going to depend on luck alone to sort out your everyday needs.

11–16: You may in fact be quite lucky but you're particularly interested in bad luck and spend too much time worrying about what bad things you assume luck must have in store for you. You have no problem believing that luck can make extra-ordinary things happen but up to now you have found it hard to imagine that these could be good or nice things.

(Oops!) So, fingers crossed . . .

I hope that this book has told you at least one thing about luck that you didn't know already. After 35 years of intensive research and study of the luck phenomenon I cannot claim to be the luckiest person in the world but I am getting luckier, I think – either that or my standards are slipping.

I figure that if you want good luck and plenty of it then the following points may help:

1 Never assume that there are any limits on when you can be lucky or how much luck you can have.

2 Expect luck to work for you and look out for ways that it does so in your life.

3

Don't decide if something is lucky or unlucky straightaway. (There are obvious exceptions to this, like trodding in dog mess which is nearly always unlucky.)

4

Don't try *too* hard.

Acknowledgements and further reading

I have found the following books a source of inspiration, ideas and stories and they would be useful to anyone wanting to read further on Luck in all its aspects.

Complete Guide to your Stars
Terri King, Element 1995

Astrological Horoscope Series (yearly guide for each sign)
Terri King, Element 1998

The Illustrated Encyclopaedia of Divination
Stephen Karcher, Element 1998

The Elements of Numerology
Rodford Barratt, Element 1994

Win the Lottery, How to pick your personal lucky numbers
Ellin Dodge, Moeller 1994

The Good Luck Book
Bill Harris, Ottenheimer 1996

The Return of Heroic Failures
Stephen Pile, Secker & Warburg 1988

Make your own luck
Seizan Fukami, Tachibana Shuppan 1994

Positively Wyrd
Tom Graves, Gothic Image 1995

Predicting
The Diagram Group, Harper Collins 1991

Practical Magic in the Northern Tradition
Nigel Pennick, The Aquarian Press 1989

Touch Wood, An Encyclopaedia of Superstition
Carole Potter, Michael O'Mara 1990

Serendipity, Accidental Discoveries in Science
Royston M Roberts, John Wiley & Sons 1989